To:

_____

From:

_____

Illustrations © 1997 by Precious Moments, Inc.
Licensee Garborg's, Inc. All rights reserved worldwide.

Text © 1997 by Garborg's, Inc.

Published by Garborg's, Inc., P.O. Box 20132, Bloomington, MN 55420

No part of this book may be reproduced in any form without permission in
writing from the publisher. All rights reserved.

Scripture quotations marked NIV are taken from the *HOLY BIBLE, NEW
INTERNATIONAL VERSION* NIV®. Copyright © 1973, 1978, 1984 by International
Bible Society. Used by permission of Zondervan Publishing House.

Scripture quotations marked NCV are taken from *The Holy Bible, New Century Version,*
copyright © 1987,1988, 1991 by Word Publishing, Dallas, Texas 75039.
Used by permission.

Scripture quotations marked TLB are taken from the *The Living Bible* © 1971. Used by
permission of Tyndale House Publishers, Inc., Wheaton, IL 60189. All rights reserved.

ISBN 1-881830-62-4

There's Nothing Sweeter Than a Friend

Everyone was meant to share God's
all-abiding love and care; He saw that we
would need to know a way to let these
feelings show.... So God made hugs.

JILL WOLF

You're my friend—
What a thing friendship is,
world without end!

ROBERT BROWNING

Our road will be smooth and untroubled
no matter what care life may send;
If we travel the pathway together,
and walk side by side with a friend.

HENRY VAN DYKE

A friend is one who loves
you as you are.

A friend knows the song
in your heart and responds
with beautiful harmony.

How many, many friendships
Life's path has let me see;
I've kept a scrap of each of them
To make the whole of me.

JUNE MASTERS BACHER

To get the full value of a joy you must
have somebody to divide it with.

MARK TWAIN

If you love someone you will be loyal
to him no matter what the cost.

1 CORINTHIANS 13:7 TLB

Friends will not only live in harmony,
but in melody.

HENRY DAVID THOREAU

Blessed are the ones God sends
to show His love for us...our friends.

Friendship is one of the
sweetest joys of life.

CHARLES H. SPURGEON

Because I have known you, my friend,
I know more of God.

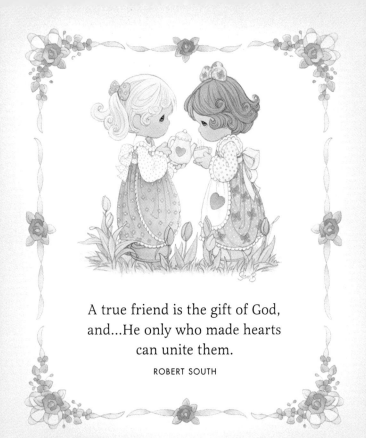

A true friend is the gift of God,
and...He only who made hearts
can unite them.

ROBERT SOUTH

My best times are the times
I spend with you!

ROY LESSIN

To love, and to be loved, is the greatest
happiness of existence.

SYDNEY SMITH

Friends are the flowers in
the garden of life.

I count myself in nothing else so happy
As in a soul remembering
my good friends.

WILLIAM SHAKESPEARE

It is always good to know, if only in passing, a charming human being; it refreshes our lives like flowers and wood and clear brooks.

GEORGE ELIOT

We are each a secret to the other.
To know one another means to feel
mutual affection and confidence,
and to believe in one another.

ALBERT SCHWEITZER

Friends...they cherish one another's
hopes. They are kind to one
another's dreams.

HENRY DAVID THOREAU

There's something beautiful
about finding one's innermost
thoughts in another.

OLIVER SCHREINER

Friends warm the world
with happiness!

Love each other...and take delight
in honoring each other.

ROMANS 12:10 TLB

Friendship is a gift from God
that's blessed in every part...
born through love and loyalty...
conceived within the heart.

The fountain of beauty is the heart,
and every generous thought illustrates
the walls of your chamber.

FRANCIS QUARLES

No love, no friendship can cross the
path of our destiny without leaving
some mark on it forever.

FRANÇOIS MAURIAC

I thank my God upon every
remembrance of you.

PHILIPPIANS 1:3 KJV

Heaven bless you...
just for being you.

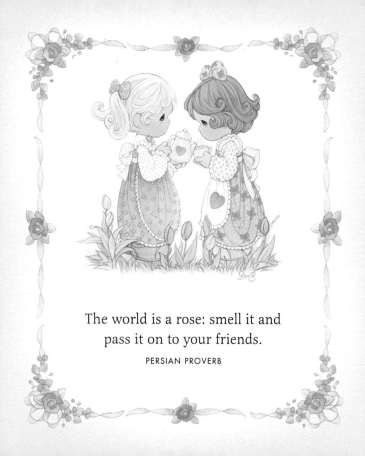

The world is a rose: smell it and
pass it on to your friends.

PERSIAN PROVERB

A friend is a person with whom
I may be sincere, before whom
I may think out loud.

RALPH WALDO EMERSON

A friend understands what you are trying to say...even when your thoughts aren't fitting into words.

ANN D. PARRISH

I thank God, my friend, for the blessing
you are...for the joy of you laughter...
the comfort of your prayers...the
warmth of your smile.

Having someone who understands is
a great blessing for ourselves. Being
someone who understands is a
great blessing to others.

JANETTE OKE

I will always keep the memories
of the special joys we have shared
close to my heart.

A friendship in which heart speaks
to heart is a gift from God.

HENRI NOUWEN

Moments shared with you
are refreshing streams
of Heaven's Light.

Friendship is sharing openly,
laughing often, trusting always,
caring deeply.

One of life's greatest treasures
is the love that binds hearts
together in friendship.

May the Lord watch between you
and me when we are absent
one from another.

GENESIS 31:49 NKJV

Love each other deeply
with all your heart.

1 PETER 1:22 NCV

How good it feels, the hand
of an old friend!

HENRY WADSWORTH LONGFELLOW

The heart of a friend is a wondrous thing,
A gift of God most fair;
For the seed of friendship there sprouts
and grows to love and beauty rare.

PAT LESSIN

Friendship is something that raised
us almost above humanity.... It is
the sort of love one can imagine
between angels.

C. S. LEWIS

Someone to talk to, to laugh with,
to tell secrets to...
I'm just so thankful for the friend
I've found in you.

Dear friends are never forgotten:
they live within your heart.

Thank you for the treasure of
your friendship...for showing me
God's special heart of love.

I appreciate your thoughtfulness and
kind ways. I appreciate all the things
you do and all the ways you
show that you care.

ROY LESSIN

Thoughtfulness is to friendship
what sunshine is to a garden.

The best and most beautiful things
in the world cannot be seen or even
touched. They must be felt
with the heart.

HELEN KELLER

Together is the nicest place to be.

Friendship is precious, not only in the
shade, but in the sunshine of life; and
thanks to a benevolent arrangement of
things, the greater part of life is sunshine.

THOMAS JEFFERSON

A friend is able to see you as
the wonderful person God
created you to be.

ANN D. PARRISH

The supreme happiness of life
is the conviction that we are loved,
loved for ourselves.

VICTOR HUGO

True friends are never far apart,
each keeps the other in her heart.

Friendship is the breathing rose,
with sweets in every fold.

OLIVER WENDELL HOLMES

To have a friend is to have one of the
sweetest gifts that life can bring.

AMY ROBERTSON BROWN

There is no joy like the joy of sharing.

BILLY GRAHAM

Friendship is not created by what
we give, but more by what we share.
It makes a whole world of
things easier to bear.

To know someone here or there
with whom you feel there is an
understanding in spite of distances
or thoughts unexpressed—that can
make of this earth a garden.

GOETHE

I will always keep the memory
of the special joys we have
shared close to my heart.

Your best friend is the person who
brings out of you the best
that is within you.

HENRY FORD

One of the highest compliments I can
receive is that I am your friend.

Be kind to one another, tenderhearted,
forgiving one another.

EPHESIANS 4:32 NRSV

Your kindness gives love
a melody, your friendship
gives memory a tune.

A friend may well be reckoned
the masterpiece of nature.

RALPH WALDO EMERSON

A friend is a precious possession
Whose value increases with the years.

HENRY VAN DYKE

I asked for happiness for you
In all things great and small.
But it was God's loving care
I prayed for most of all.

The song of our friendship
is a melody only our
hearts can sing.

Oh, the comfort, the inexpressible comfort of feeling safe with a person: having neither to weigh thoughts nor measure words, but to pour them out.

GEORGE ELIOT

A friend loves at all times.

PROVERBS 17:17 NKJV

Friends believe in your dreams
as much as you do.

My friend is one who takes me
for who I am.

HENRY DAVID THOREAU

Whenever I think of you,
I smile inside.

May happiness touch your life today
as warmly as you have touched
the lives of others.

Only a life lived for others
is worthwhile.

ALBERT EINSTEIN

You are a blessing sent from Heaven
above, a huggable reminder of
God's unfailing love.

My heart is content with just knowing
Fulfillment that true friendship brings;
It fills to the brim, overflowing
With pleasure in life's "little things."

JUNE MASTERS BACHER

Blessed is the influence of one true,
loving human soul on another.

GEORGE ELIOT

Friendships begun in this world
can be taken up again in heaven,
never to be broken off.

ST. FRANCIS DE SALES

Among God's best gifts to us are
the people who love us.

A cup of tea, a prayer or two,
blessed moments shared with you.

ELLEN CUOMO

Our lives are filled with simple joys
and blessings without end
And one of the greatest joys in life
is to have a friend.

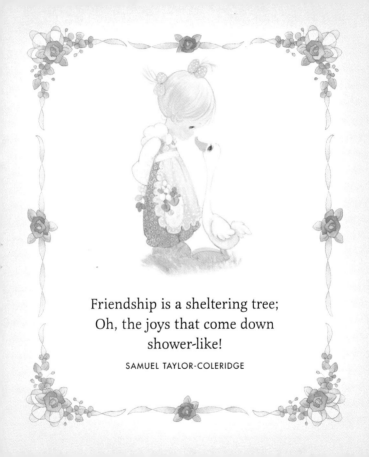

Friendship is a sheltering tree;
Oh, the joys that come down
shower-like!

SAMUEL TAYLOR-COLERIDGE

Hand
Grasps hand, eye lights eye
in good friendship,
And great hearts expand,
And grow one in the sense of
this world's life.

ROBERT BROWNING

One whose grip is a little tighter,
One whose smile is a little brighter,
One whose deeds are a little whiter,
That's what I call a friend.

JOHN BURROUGHS

A lasting friendship is a treasure.

Encourage each other to
build each other up.

1 THESSALONIANS 5:11 TLB

Two are better than one....
For if they fall, one will
lift up the other.

ECCLESIASTES 4:9,10 NRSV

We have not made ourselves;
we are the gift of the living
God to one another.

REINE DUELL BETHANY

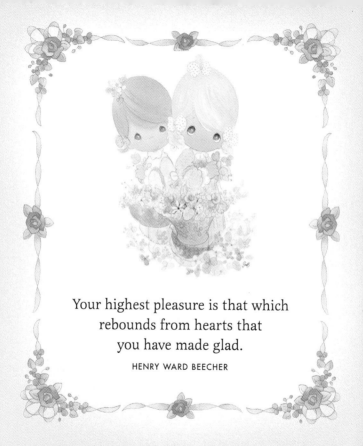

Your highest pleasure is that which
rebounds from hearts that
you have made glad.

HENRY WARD BEECHER

I am so glad you are here....
It helps me to realize how
beautiful my world is.

RAINER MARIA RILKE

Now may the warming love of friends
surround you as you go
Down the path of light and laughter
where the happy memories grow.

HELEN LOWRIE MARSHALL

My friend shall forever be my friend,
and reflect a ray of God to me.

HENRY DAVID THOREAU

A friend is the hope of the heart.

RALPH WALDO EMERSON

While friends are near us, we feel that
all is well.... Our everyday life blossoms
suddenly into bright possibilities.

HELEN KELLER

Friends are the sunshine of life.
When friends meet, hearts warm.

JOHN RAY

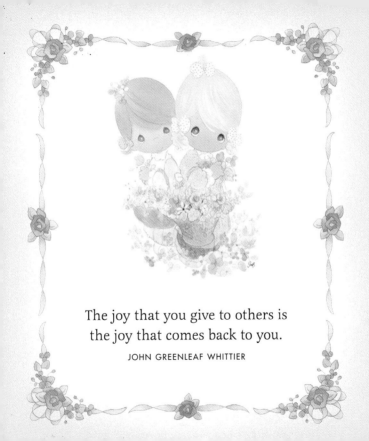

The joy that you give to others is
the joy that comes back to you.

JOHN GREENLEAF WHITTIER

Joy is the echo of God's life within us.

JOSEPH MARMION

Every true friend is a glimpse of God.

· LUCY LARCOM

Happiness is my friend's hand.

GILLIAN QUEEN, AGE 10

A friend is what the heart
needs all the time.

HENRY VAN DYKE